This book belongs to...

_____

Be Prepared For Anything

Love Yourself First

Today I Am Grateful For...

This worksheet is designed to help you practice gratitude. Make as many copies as you'd like. The more you practice gratitude, the happier your life will be.

Something that happened to me recently that I am grateful for:
_____
_____
_____
_____
_____
_____
_____

Someone who is always there for me and I really appreciate:
_____
_____
_____

Someone I look up to and why:
_____
_____
_____
_____
_____
_____

The best thing that happened today:
_____
_____
_____
_____

Something that has made my life easier:
_____
_____
_____
_____
_____
_____

Someone I love spending time with and why:
_____
_____
_____
_____
_____
_____

I smiled or belly laughed today because:
_____
_____
_____
_____
_____
_____

A song that makes me happy
_____
_____

Something I was able to do for someone else that made me happy:
_____
_____
_____

Something that has changed my life for the better in the past year and how it has impacted my life.
_____
_____
_____
_____
_____
_____
_____
_____
_____

I'm looking forward to:
_____
_____
_____
_____
_____
_____

Simple pleasures I enjoy:
_____
_____
_____
_____

Something or someone that has inspired me and how:
_____
_____
_____
_____
_____
_____
_____

Positive Thinking To Help Situational Depression

Negativity is often an overwhelming element of situational depression. For millions of people with this type of depression, the key to begin breaking free is to change the situation, when possible, and/or the way the situation is viewed.

What situation is contributing to or causing my depression?
_____
_____
_____
_____

Is the situation a result of my actions or choices? Explain.
_____
_____
_____
_____

What are the positive things I've learned due the experience?
_____
_____
_____
_____

If I could do it over again, this is what I would do differently:
_____
_____
_____

Is negative self-talk making my depression worse? Give examples:

_____
_____
_____
_____

I can change the negative thoughts and self-talk into positives like these:

_____
_____
_____
_____

I can alleviate my stress and depression by focusing on the positives such as:

_____
_____
_____
_____

When situations are not a result of my actions or choices and I have limited control over things, I need to take these steps to maintain a positive mindset:

_____
_____
_____
_____

If I need additional help staying positive or fighting back the depression, I can count on and contact these friends and professionals:

_____
_____
_____

25 Positive Thinking Affirmations

Affirmations are simple reminders to our subconscious that tells it to stay positive and focused on reaching our goals. They are meant to be used for ourselves, not for others. Affirmations can create more appreciation for the things we have and are surrounded with. They can bring more joy and happiness to our lives.

When creating your affirmations, there are a few things to keep in mind.

- Including the words "I am" in your affirmations bring power to your statement.
- Positively state what you want, not what you don't want.
- Keep your statements short and specific.
- Include words that show action or emotion
- Before stating your affirmation, take a deep breath and focus on what you're saying.
- Be grateful for what you have, the people in your life and your surroundings.
- Let go of the past. You can't change it so don't waste time thinking on it.
- Celebrate your 'wins'.

Below are 25 positive thinking affirmations to get you started.

1. I can do better, just by deciding to do so.
2. Life is what I make of it.
3. I can.
4. I am above negative thoughts and actions.
5. Happiness is a choice. I choose it.
6. Today, I let go of old habits and take up new ones.
7. I am conquering obstacles every day.
8. I am seeing a positive in every situation.
9. My thoughts are becoming more positive each day.
10. Life is getting better all the time.
11. I am turning into the person I always wanted to be.
12. Thinking positive is starting to feel more natural to me.
13. My optimism is altering my reality.
14. I am at peace with my past and looking forward to the future.
15. I no longer fear tomorrow.
16. I am blessed.
17. This too shall pass.
18. I control how I feel.
19. I am willing to do what it takes to make positive changes.
20. The future is mine, if I choose to take it.
21. I am indestructible.
22. This moment is awesome.
23. Positive thinking is part of who I am now.
24. Today is the first day of my new life.
25. Everything happens for a reason that serves me.

Every step that I take to move forward allows me to grow stronger by the day.

30 Ways to Think More Positively

After years of having a fixed, negative mindset, it's tough to change one's ways. But with practice, you can create a more positive outlook on life. Here's 30 ways to practice thinking more positively.

1. When talking, replace negative words with positive words. Instead of saying "This is too hard", say "I can do this" or "I accept this challenge".

2. When thinking, use empowering words; those that make you feel strong, happy, motivated and in control.

3. Journal your thoughts. Celebrate your successes. Document and analyze the losses. Find where you went wrong and plan to do better next time. Learn from your mistakes.

4. Counter each negative thought with multiple positive thoughts. When you catch yourself having negative thoughts, take a moment to think two or three positive thoughts.

5. Go somewhere that brings you peace and happiness. This might be a nature walk, a quiet place like a museum that is visually appealing, an area where you listen to music, a park where you can watch kids and pets play happily. As often as possible, visit this place where you feel peace and happiness.

6. Practice positive affirmations. The more you practice, the easier it will become.

7. Forgive yourself for missteps. It happens. The important this is not to dwell on them and keep moving forward.

8. Surround yourself with positive people.

9. Add inspiring visuals and colors to your home and work space.

10. Look at things from a different point of view. When you can see both sides, you can eliminate a lot of negatively.

11. Laugh aloud and often. There's always something to laugh about. Smiling and laughing releases 'feel good' endorphins in the body.

12. Remember your "why". Why you are trying to be more positive, what your goals are, how things will be better once you meet your goals, etc.

13. Practice gratitude. When you're feeling thankful, you'll feel more positive.

14. Live in the moment. Stop worrying about yesterday or what's coming. Do what you can do today to get one step closer to reaching your goals.

15. Indulge yourself occasionally. You are working hard to be a more positive person. You deserve a small reward.

16. Carry a funny photo with you. Save a funny video on your phone to give you a boost when you're feeling down.

17. Look at each challenge as an opportunity to grow. Strive for excellence.

18. Relax. Sometimes you just need to step back, breathe deep and relax to get the good vibes flowing again.

19. Get physically active to release more 'feel good' endorphins.

20. Believe in yourself. The only thing keeping you from succeeding is your own negative thoughts. Stop getting in your own way.

21. Stop making excuses and laying blame. Take responsibility for your actions and make the choice to do better next time.

22. Observe your thought patterns. Are there certain times of the day when you're feeling more negative? What can you do to make those times more positive?

23. Ask yourself, does this really matter? Will it matter next week or next month? If not, let it go. This called not sweating the small stuff.

24. Practice proper posture. Standing or sitting up with the back straight, shoulders back and chin up will help the mind and body feel better.

25. Be kind to others. Compliment a stranger. Do something nice for coworker or friend. Call a family member you haven't talked to in a while.

26. Read something inspiring every day. Follow those who inspire you most and see what they do each day to make like the best it can be. Follow their lead.

27. Dance and sing. It doesn't matter if you have two left feet or can't carry a tune. Crank up the music and give it all you've got.

28. Look for the positive. Even in the worst of situations, there's always something positive if you just look for it.

29. Have a personal mantra. No matter what it is, these will be the words you live by each day that reminds you to be positive.

30. Meditate, do yoga, concentrate on your breathing and relaxing your mind.

Challenges I Will Overcome

Life is full of challenges. This worksheet is designed to help you work through how you'll overcome the challenges you face.

The Challenge I'm Currently Facing

_____
_____
_____
_____
_____

The Obstacle(s) Standing in My Way

Obstacle #1:
_____
_____

How I Will Overcome It
_____
_____
_____
_____

People & Tools I'll Need to Help Me with This
_____
_____
_____

Obstacle #2:
_____

How I Will Overcome It
_____
_____
_____
_____

People & Tools I'll Need to Help Me with This
_____
_____
_____
_____

Obstacle #3:
_____
_____

How I Will Overcome It
_____
_____
_____
_____

People & Tools I'll Need to Help Me with This
_____
_____
_____
_____

Previous Challenges That May Resurface & How I Will Handle Them
_____
_____
_____

Previous Challenges That May Resurface & How I Will Handle Them

More Thoughts on This Challenge:

Top Characteristics of Happy People

Ever wonder why some people always seem happy when others do not? It's all about how you view things. Below are the top characteristics of happy people.

Happy people:

- Practice gratitude and show their appreciation.
- Are genuinely nice to others
- Are open and honest
- Are cooperative
- Smile when they mean it
- Are well-adjusted and appreciate simple pleasures
- Surround themselves with other happy people
- Are spontaneous and adventurous
- Are good listeners
- Have fewer expectations, and fewer disappointments
- Don't judge others and don't let judgmental people affect them.
- Actively try to be happy each day
- Are resilient. They bounce back from obstacles and failures.
- Help others when they can
- Spend time doing nothing
- Choose meaningful conversations over small talk
- Stay connected with those they love
- Look for the positive in everything
- Regularly unplug from technology, if only for a few hours a week.
- Try to maintain a healthy mind and body through proper eating, exercise, and rest.

- Laugh loud and laugh often, fully enjoying the moment
- Like themselves
- Have self-control
- Are optimistic
- Are spiritual
- Lead a balanced life
- Embrace their creativity

S.M.A.R.T. Goals Worksheet

Goals give us something to visualize, to work towards. They keep us from becoming stagnant in life. This worksheet is designed to help you set smart goals.

Today's Date: _____   Date to Achieve Goal By: _____

                                     Date Goal Achieved: _____

Specific: What exactly do you want to accomplish? What is the desired result. Why do you want to achieve it? How do you plan to achieve it? Be specific.

_____
_____
_____
_____
_____
_____
_____
_____
_____
_____
_____
_____
_____
_____
_____
_____
_____
_____
_____

Measurable: How will you know when you've accomplished this goal? How are you going to measure your progress? How often are you going to measure and document your progress?

_____
_____
_____
_____
_____
_____
_____
_____
_____
_____
_____

Achievable: Is this goal achievable? What skills, tools, and resources do you need to make it happen? Do you have these? If not, how will you get them?

_____
_____
_____
_____
_____
_____
_____
_____
_____
_____
_____

Relevant: Is this goal relevant to your life? Will it help you reach your life goals quicker? Will it benefit your life in some way? How is it relevant? Be specific.

_____
_____
_____
_____
_____
_____
_____
_____
_____
_____

Timely: When do you want to achieve this goal? Is this target date reasonable?

_____
_____
_____

Progress / Notes

Month 1	Month 2	Month 3	Month 4	Month 5	Month 6

Every step that I take to move forward allows me to grow stronger by the day.

Today I Am Grateful For...

This worksheet is designed to help you practice gratitude. Make as many copies as you'd like. The more you practice gratitude, the happier your life will be.

Something that happened to me recently that I am grateful for:
_____
_____
_____
_____
_____
_____
_____

Someone who is always there for me and I really appreciate:
_____
_____
_____

Someone I look up to and why:
_____
_____
_____
_____
_____
_____

The best thing that happened today:
_____
_____
_____
_____

Something that has made my life easier:
_____
_____
_____
_____
_____
_____

Someone I love spending time with and why:
_____
_____
_____
_____
_____
_____

I smiled or belly laughed today because:
_____
_____
_____
_____
_____
_____

A song that makes me happy
_____
_____

Something I was able to do for someone else that made me happy:
_____
_____
_____

Something that has changed my life for the better in the past year and how it has impacted my life.
_____
_____
_____
_____
_____
_____
_____
_____

I'm looking forward to:
_____
_____
_____
_____
_____
_____

Simple pleasures I enjoy:
_____
_____
_____
_____

Something or someone that has inspired me and how:
_____
_____
_____
_____
_____
_____
_____
_____

Positive Thinking To Help Situational Depression

Negativity is often an overwhelming element of situational depression. For millions of people with this type of depression, the key to begin breaking free is to change the situation, when possible, and/or the way the situation is viewed.

What situation is contributing to or causing my depression?
_____
_____
_____
_____

Is the situation a result of my actions or choices? Explain.
_____
_____
_____
_____

What are the positive things I've learned due the experience?
_____
_____
_____
_____

If I could do it over again, this is what I would do differently:
_____
_____
_____

Is negative self-talk making my depression worse? Give examples:
_____
_____
_____
_____

I can change the negative thoughts and self-talk into positives like these:
_____
_____
_____
_____

I can alleviate my stress and depression by focusing on the positives such as:
_____
_____
_____
_____

When situations are not a result of my actions or choices and I have limited control over things, I need to take these steps to maintain a positive mindset:
_____
_____
_____
_____

If I need additional help staying positive or fighting back the depression, I can count on and contact these friends and professionals:
_____
_____

25 Positive Thinking Affirmations

Affirmations are simple reminders to our subconscious that tells it to stay positive and focused on reaching our goals. They are meant to be used for ourselves, not for others. Affirmations can create more appreciation for the things we have and are surrounded with. They can bring more joy and happiness to our lives.

When creating your affirmations, there are a few things to keep in mind.

- Including the words "I am" in your affirmations bring power to your statement.
- Positively state what you want, not what you don't want.
- Keep your statements short and specific.
- Include words that show action or emotion
- Before stating your affirmation, take a deep breath and focus on what you're saying.
- Be grateful for what you have, the people in your life and your surroundings.
- Let go of the past. You can't change it so don't waste time thinking on it.
- Celebrate your 'wins'.

Below are 25 positive thinking affirmations to get you started.

1. I can do better, just by deciding to do so.
2. Life is what I make of it.
3. I can.
4. I am above negative thoughts and actions.
5. Happiness is a choice. I choose it.
6. Today, I let go of old habits and take up new ones.
7. I am conquering obstacles every day.
8. I am seeing a positive in every situation.
9. My thoughts are becoming more positive each day.
10. Life is getting better all the time.
11. I am turning into the person I always wanted to be.
12. Thinking positive is starting to feel more natural to me.
13. My optimism is altering my reality.
14. I am at peace with my past and looking forward to the future.
15. I no longer fear tomorrow.
16. I am blessed.
17. This too shall pass.
18. I control how I feel.
19. I am willing to do what it takes to make positive changes.
20. The future is mine, if I choose to take it.
21. I am indestructible.
22. This moment is awesome.
23. Positive thinking is part of who I am now.
24. Today is the first day of my new life.
25. Everything happens for a reason that serves me.

Every step that I take to move forward allows me to grow stronger by the day.

30 Ways to Think More Positively

After years of having a fixed, negative mindset, it's tough to change one's ways. But with practice, you can create a more positive outlook on life. Here's 30 ways to practice thinking more positively.

1. When talking, replace negative words with positive words. Instead of saying "This is too hard", say "I can do this" or "I accept this challenge".

2. When thinking, use empowering words; those that make you feel strong, happy, motivated and in control.

3. Journal your thoughts. Celebrate your successes. Document and analyze the losses. Find where you went wrong and plan to do better next time. Learn from your mistakes.

4. Counter each negative thought with multiple positive thoughts. When you catch yourself having negative thoughts, take a moment to think two or three positive thoughts.

5. Go somewhere that brings you peace and happiness. This might be a nature walk, a quiet place like a museum that is visually appealing, an area where you listen to music, a park where you can watch kids and pets play happily. As often as possible, visit this place where you feel peace and happiness.

6. Practice positive affirmations. The more you practice, the easier it will become.

7. Forgive yourself for missteps. It happens. The important this is not to dwell on them and keep moving forward.

8. Surround yourself with positive people.

9. Add inspiring visuals and colors to your home and work space.

10. Look at things from a different point of view. When you can see both sides, you can eliminate a lot of negatively.

11. Laugh aloud and often. There's always something to laugh about. Smiling and laughing releases 'feel good' endorphins in the body.

12. Remember your "why". Why you are trying to be more positive, what your goals are, how things will be better once you meet your goals, etc.

13. Practice gratitude. When you're feeling thankful, you'll feel more positive.

14. Live in the moment. Stop worrying about yesterday or what's coming. Do what you can do today to get one step closer to reaching your goals.

15. Indulge yourself occasionally. You are working hard to be a more positive person. You deserve a small reward.

16. Carry a funny photo with you. Save a funny video on your phone to give you a boost when you're feeling down.

17. Look at each challenge as an opportunity to grow. Strive for excellence.

18. Relax. Sometimes you just need to step back, breathe deep and relax to get the good vibes flowing again.

19. Get physically active to release more 'feel good' endorphins.

20. Believe in yourself. The only thing keeping you from succeeding is your own negative thoughts. Stop getting in your own way.

21. Stop making excuses and laying blame. Take responsibility for your actions and make the choice to do better next time.

22. Observe your thought patterns. Are there certain times of the day when you're feeling more negative? What can you do to make those times more positive?

23. Ask yourself, does this really matter? Will it matter next week or next month? If not, let it go. This called not sweating the small stuff.

24. Practice proper posture. Standing or sitting up with the back straight, shoulders back and chin up will help the mind and body feel better.

25. Be kind to others. Compliment a stranger. Do something nice for coworker or friend. Call a family member you haven't talked to in a while.

26. Read something inspiring every day. Follow those who inspire you most and see what they do each day to make like the best it can be. Follow their lead.

27. Dance and sing. It doesn't matter if you have two left feet or can't carry a tune. Crank up the music and give it all you've got.

28. Look for the positive. Even in the worst of situations, there's always something positive if you just look for it.

29. Have a personal mantra. No matter what it is, these will be the words you live by each day that reminds you to be positive.

30. Meditate, do yoga, concentrate on your breathing and relaxing your mind.

Challenges I Will Overcome

Life is full of challenges. This worksheet is designed to help you work through how you'll overcome the challenges you face.

The Challenge I'm Currently Facing

_____
_____
_____
_____
_____

The Obstacle(s) Standing in My Way

Obstacle #1:

_____
_____

How I Will Overcome It

_____
_____
_____
_____

People & Tools I'll Need to Help Me with This

_____
_____
_____
_____

Obstacle #2:

_____

How I Will Overcome It

_____
_____
_____
_____

People & Tools I'll Need to Help Me with This

_____
_____
_____
_____

Obstacle #3:

_____
_____

How I Will Overcome It

_____
_____
_____
_____

People & Tools I'll Need to Help Me with This

_____
_____
_____
_____

Previous Challenges That May Resurface & How I Will Handle Them

_____
_____
_____

_____
_____

Previous Challenges That May Resurface & How I Will Handle Them
_____
_____
_____
_____
_____
_____
_____
_____

More Thoughts on This Challenge:
_____
_____
_____
_____
_____
_____
_____
_____
_____
_____
_____
_____
_____

Top Characteristics of Happy People

Ever wonder why some people always seem happy when others do not? It's all about how you view things. Below are the top characteristics of happy people.

Happy people:

- Practice gratitude and show their appreciation.
- Are genuinely nice to others
- Are open and honest
- Are cooperative
- Smile when they mean it
- Are well-adjusted and appreciate simple pleasures
- Surround themselves with other happy people
- Are spontaneous and adventurous
- Are good listeners
- Have fewer expectations, and fewer disappointments
- Don't judge others and don't let judgmental people affect them.
- Actively try to be happy each day
- Are resilient. They bounce back from obstacles and failures.
- Help others when they can
- Spend time doing nothing
- Choose meaningful conversations over small talk
- Stay connected with those they love
- Look for the positive in everything
- Regularly unplug from technology, if only for a few hours a week.
- Try to maintain a healthy mind and body through proper eating, exercise, and rest.

- Laugh loud and laugh often, fully enjoying the moment
- Like themselves
- Have self-control
- Are optimistic
- Are spiritual
- Lead a balanced life
- Embrace their creativity

S.M.A.R.T. Goals Worksheet

Goals give us something to visualize, to work towards. They keep us from becoming stagnant in life. This worksheet is designed to help you set smart goals.

Today's Date: _____   Date to Achieve Goal By: _____

　　　　　　　　　　　　　　　　　　　　　Date Goal Achieved: _____

Specific: What exactly do you want to accomplish? What is the desired result. Why do you want to achieve it? How do you plan to achieve it? Be specific.

_____
_____
_____
_____
_____
_____
_____
_____
_____
_____
_____
_____
_____
_____
_____
_____
_____
_____
_____
_____

Measurable: How will you know when you've accomplished this goal? How are you going to measure your progress? How often are you going to measure and document your progress?

_____
_____
_____
_____
_____
_____
_____
_____
_____
_____
_____
_____

Achievable: Is this goal achievable? What skills, tools, and resources do you need to make it happen? Do you have these? If not, how will you get them?

_____
_____
_____
_____
_____
_____
_____
_____
_____
_____
_____
_____

Relevant: Is this goal relevant to your life? Will it help you reach your life goals quicker? Will it benefit your life in some way? How is it relevant? Be specific.

_____
_____
_____
_____
_____
_____
_____
_____
_____
_____

Timely: When do you want to achieve this goal? Is this target date reasonable?

_____
_____
_____

Progress / Notes

Month 1	Month 2	Month 3	Month 4	Month 5	Month 6

Every step that I take to move forward allows me to grow stronger by the day.

Today I Am Grateful For...

This worksheet is designed to help you practice gratitude. Make as many copies as you'd like. The more you practice gratitude, the happier your life will be.

Something that happened to me recently that I am grateful for:
_____
_____
_____
_____
_____
_____
_____

Someone who is always there for me and I really appreciate:
_____
_____
_____

Someone I look up to and why:
_____
_____
_____
_____
_____
_____

The best thing that happened today:
_____
_____
_____
_____

Something that has made my life easier:
_____
_____
_____
_____
_____
_____

Someone I love spending time with and why:
_____
_____
_____
_____
_____
_____

I smiled or belly laughed today because:
_____
_____
_____
_____
_____
_____

A song that makes me happy
_____
_____

Something I was able to do for someone else that made me happy:
_____
_____
_____

Something that has changed my life for the better in the past year and how it has impacted my life.
_____
_____
_____
_____
_____
_____
_____
_____
_____

I'm looking forward to:
_____
_____
_____
_____
_____
_____

Simple pleasures I enjoy:
_____
_____
_____
_____

Something or someone that has inspired me and how:
_____
_____
_____
_____
_____
_____
_____
_____

Positive Thinking To Help Situational Depression

Negativity is often an overwhelming element of situational depression. For millions of people with this type of depression, the key to begin breaking free is to change the situation, when possible, and/or the way the situation is viewed.

What situation is contributing to or causing my depression?
_____
_____
_____
_____

Is the situation a result of my actions or choices? Explain.
_____
_____
_____
_____

What are the positive things I've learned due the experience?
_____
_____
_____
_____

If I could do it over again, this is what I would do differently:
_____
_____
_____

Is negative self-talk making my depression worse? Give examples:

_____
_____
_____
_____

I can change the negative thoughts and self-talk into positives like these:

_____
_____
_____
_____

I can alleviate my stress and depression by focusing on the positives such as:

_____
_____
_____
_____

When situations are not a result of my actions or choices and I have limited control over things, I need to take these steps to maintain a positive mindset:

_____
_____
_____
_____

If I need additional help staying positive or fighting back the depression, I can count on and contact these friends and professionals:

_____
_____
_____

25 Positive Thinking Affirmations

Affirmations are simple reminders to our subconscious that tells it to stay positive and focused on reaching our goals. They are meant to be used for ourselves, not for others. Affirmations can create more appreciation for the things we have and are surrounded with. They can bring more joy and happiness to our lives.

When creating your affirmations, there are a few things to keep in mind.

- Including the words "I am" in your affirmations bring power to your statement.
- Positively state what you want, not what you don't want.
- Keep your statements short and specific.
- Include words that show action or emotion
- Before stating your affirmation, take a deep breath and focus on what you're saying.
- Be grateful for what you have, the people in your life and your surroundings.
- Let go of the past. You can't change it so don't waste time thinking on it.
- Celebrate your 'wins'.

Below are 25 positive thinking affirmations to get you started.

26. I can do better, just by deciding to do so.
27. Life is what I make of it.
28. I can.
29. I am above negative thoughts and actions.
30. Happiness is a choice. I choose it.
31. Today, I let go of old habits and take up new ones.
32. I am conquering obstacles every day.
33. I am seeing a positive in every situation.
34. My thoughts are becoming more positive each day.
35. Life is getting better all the time.
36. I am turning into the person I always wanted to be.
37. Thinking positive is starting to feel more natural to me.
38. My optimism is altering my reality.
39. I am at peace with my past and looking forward to the future.
40. I no longer fear tomorrow.
41. I am blessed.
42. This too shall pass.
43. I control how I feel.
44. I am willing to do what it takes to make positive changes.
45. The future is mine, if I choose to take it.
46. I am indestructible.
47. This moment is awesome.
48. Positive thinking is part of who I am now.
49. Today is the first day of my new life.
50. Everything happens for a reason that serves me.

Every step that I take to move forward allows me to grow stronger by the day.

30 Ways to Think More Positively

After years of having a fixed, negative mindset, it's tough to change one's ways. But with practice, you can create a more positive outlook on life. Here's 30 ways to practice thinking more positively.

1. When talking, replace negative words with positive words. Instead of saying "This is too hard", say "I can do this" or "I accept this challenge".

2. When thinking, use empowering words; those that make you feel strong, happy, motivated and in control.

3. Journal your thoughts. Celebrate your successes. Document and analyze the losses. Find where you went wrong and plan to do better next time. Learn from your mistakes.

4. Counter each negative thought with multiple positive thoughts. When you catch yourself having negative thoughts, take a moment to think two or three positive thoughts.

5. Go somewhere that brings you peace and happiness. This might be a nature walk, a quiet place like a museum that is visually appealing, an area where you listen to music, a park where you can watch kids and pets play happily. As often as possible, visit this place where you feel peace and happiness.

6. Practice positive affirmations. The more you practice, the easier it will become.

7. Forgive yourself for missteps. It happens. The important this is not to dwell on them and keep moving forward.

8. Surround yourself with positive people.

9. Add inspiring visuals and colors to your home and work space.

10. Look at things from a different point of view. When you can see both sides, you can eliminate a lot of negatively.

11. Laugh aloud and often. There's always something to laugh about. Smiling and laughing releases 'feel good' endorphins in the body.

12. Remember your "why". Why you are trying to be more positive, what your goals are, how things will be better once you meet your goals, etc.

13. Practice gratitude. When you're feeling thankful, you'll feel more positive.

14. Live in the moment. Stop worrying about yesterday or what's coming. Do what you can do today to get one step closer to reaching your goals.

15. Indulge yourself occasionally. You are working hard to be a more positive person. You deserve a small reward.

16. Carry a funny photo with you. Save a funny video on your phone to give you a boost when you're feeling down.

17. Look at each challenge as an opportunity to grow. Strive for excellence.

18. Relax. Sometimes you just need to step back, breathe deep and relax to get the good vibes flowing again.

19. Get physically active to release more 'feel good' endorphins.

20. Believe in yourself. The only thing keeping you from succeeding is your own negative thoughts. Stop getting in your own way.

21. Stop making excuses and laying blame. Take responsibility for your actions and make the choice to do better next time.

22. Observe your thought patterns. Are there certain times of the day when you're feeling more negative? What can you do to make those times more positive?

23. Ask yourself, does this really matter? Will it matter next week or next month? If not, let it go. This called not sweating the small stuff.

24. Practice proper posture. Standing or sitting up with the back straight, shoulders back and chin up will help the mind and body feel better.

25. Be kind to others. Compliment a stranger. Do something nice for coworker or friend. Call a family member you haven't talked to in a while.

26. Read something inspiring every day. Follow those who inspire you most and see what they do each day to make like the best it can be. Follow their lead.

27. Dance and sing. It doesn't matter if you have two left feet or can't carry a tune. Crank up the music and give it all you've got.

28. Look for the positive. Even in the worst of situations, there's always something positive if you just look for it.

29. Have a personal mantra. No matter what it is, these will be the words you live by each day that reminds you to be positive.

30. Meditate, do yoga, concentrate on your breathing and relaxing your mind.

Challenges I Will Overcome

Life is full of challenges. This worksheet is designed to help you work through how you'll overcome the challenges you face.

The Challenge I'm Currently Facing

_____
_____
_____
_____
_____

The Obstacle(s) Standing in My Way

Obstacle #1:

_____
_____

How I Will Overcome It

_____
_____
_____
_____

People & Tools I'll Need to Help Me with This

_____
_____
_____
_____

Obstacle #2:

_____

How I Will Overcome It

_____
_____
_____
_____

People & Tools I'll Need to Help Me with This

_____
_____
_____
_____

Obstacle #3:

_____
_____

How I Will Overcome It

_____
_____
_____
_____

People & Tools I'll Need to Help Me with This

_____
_____
_____
_____

Previous Challenges That May Resurface & How I Will Handle Them

_____
_____
_____

Previous Challenges That May Resurface & How I Will Handle Them

More Thoughts on This Challenge:

Top Characteristics of Happy People

Ever wonder why some people always seem happy when others do not? It's all about how you view things. Below are the top characteristics of happy people.

Happy people:

- Practice gratitude and show their appreciation.
- Are genuinely nice to others
- Are open and honest
- Are cooperative
- Smile when they mean it
- Are well-adjusted and appreciate simple pleasures
- Surround themselves with other happy people
- Are spontaneous and adventurous
- Are good listeners
- Have fewer expectations, and fewer disappointments
- Don't judge others and don't let judgmental people affect them.
- Actively try to be happy each day
- Are resilient. They bounce back from obstacles and failures.
- Help others when they can
- Spend time doing nothing
- Choose meaningful conversations over small talk
- Stay connected with those they love
- Look for the positive in everything
- Regularly unplug from technology, if only for a few hours a week.
- Try to maintain a healthy mind and body through proper eating, exercise, and rest.

- Laugh loud and laugh often, fully enjoying the moment
- Like themselves
- Have self-control
- Are optimistic
- Are spiritual
- Lead a balanced life
- Embrace their creativity

S.M.A.R.T. Goals Worksheet

Goals give us something to visualize, to work towards. They keep us from becoming stagnant in life. This worksheet is designed to help you set smart goals.

Today's Date: _____   Date to Achieve Goal By: _____

                                                               Date Goal Achieved: _____

Specific: What exactly do you want to accomplish? What is the desired result. Why do you want to achieve it? How do you plan to achieve it? Be specific.

_____
_____
_____
_____
_____
_____
_____
_____
_____
_____
_____
_____
_____
_____
_____
_____
_____
_____
_____
_____

Measurable: How will you know when you've accomplished this goal? How are you going to measure your progress? How often are you going to measure and document your progress?

_____
_____
_____
_____
_____
_____
_____
_____
_____
_____
_____

Achievable: Is this goal achievable? What skills, tools, and resources do you need to make it happen? Do you have these? If not, how will you get them?

_____
_____
_____
_____
_____
_____
_____
_____
_____
_____
_____

Relevant: Is this goal relevant to your life? Will it help you reach your life goals quicker? Will it benefit your life in some way? How is it relevant? Be specific.

_____
_____
_____
_____
_____
_____
_____
_____
_____
_____

Timely: When do you want to achieve this goal? Is this target date reasonable?

_____
_____
_____

Progress / Notes

Month 1	Month 2	Month 3	Month 4	Month 5	Month 6

Every step that I take to move forward allows me to grow stronger by the day.

Today I Am Grateful For...

This worksheet is designed to help you practice gratitude. Make as many copies as you'd like. The more you practice gratitude, the happier your life will be.

Something that happened to me recently that I am grateful for:
_____
_____
_____
_____
_____
_____
_____

Someone who is always there for me and I really appreciate:
_____
_____
_____

Someone I look up to and why:
_____
_____
_____
_____
_____
_____

The best thing that happened today:
_____
_____
_____
_____

Something that has made my life easier:
_____
_____
_____
_____
_____
_____

Someone I love spending time with and why:
_____
_____
_____
_____
_____
_____

I smiled or belly laughed today because:
_____
_____
_____
_____
_____
_____

A song that makes me happy
_____
_____

Something I was able to do for someone else that made me happy:
_____
_____
_____

Something that has changed my life for the better in the past year and how it has impacted my life.
_____
_____
_____
_____
_____
_____
_____
_____
_____

I'm looking forward to:
_____
_____
_____
_____
_____
_____

Simple pleasures I enjoy:
_____
_____
_____
_____

Something or someone that has inspired me and how:
_____
_____
_____
_____
_____
_____
_____
_____

Positive Thinking To Help Situational Depression

Negativity is often an overwhelming element of situational depression. For millions of people with this type of depression, the key to begin breaking free is to change the situation, when possible, and/or the way the situation is viewed.

What situation is contributing to or causing my depression?
_____
_____
_____
_____

Is the situation a result of my actions or choices? Explain.
_____
_____
_____
_____

What are the positive things I've learned due the experience?
_____
_____
_____
_____

If I could do it over again, this is what I would do differently:
_____
_____
_____

Is negative self-talk making my depression worse? Give examples:

_____
_____
_____
_____

I can change the negative thoughts and self-talk into positives like these:

_____
_____
_____
_____

I can alleviate my stress and depression by focusing on the positives such as:

_____
_____
_____
_____

When situations are not a result of my actions or choices and I have limited control over things, I need to take these steps to maintain a positive mindset:

_____
_____
_____
_____

If I need additional help staying positive or fighting back the depression, I can count on and contact these friends and professionals:

_____
_____

25 Positive Thinking Affirmations

Affirmations are simple reminders to our subconscious that tells it to stay positive and focused on reaching our goals. They are meant to be used for ourselves, not for others. Affirmations can create more appreciation for the things we have and are surrounded with. They can bring more joy and happiness to our lives.

When creating your affirmations, there are a few things to keep in mind.

- Including the words "I am" in your affirmations bring power to your statement.
- Positively state what you want, not what you don't want.
- Keep your statements short and specific.
- Include words that show action or emotion
- Before stating your affirmation, take a deep breath and focus on what you're saying.
- Be grateful for what you have, the people in your life and your surroundings.
- Let go of the past. You can't change it so don't waste time thinking on it.
- Celebrate your 'wins'.

Below are 25 positive thinking affirmations to get you started.

1. I can do better, just by deciding to do so.
2. Life is what I make of it.
3. I can.
4. I am above negative thoughts and actions.
5. Happiness is a choice. I choose it.
6. Today, I let go of old habits and take up new ones.
7. I am conquering obstacles every day.
8. I am seeing a positive in every situation.
9. My thoughts are becoming more positive each day.
10. Life is getting better all the time.
11. I am turning into the person I always wanted to be.
12. Thinking positive is starting to feel more natural to me.
13. My optimism is altering my reality.
14. I am at peace with my past and looking forward to the future.
15. I no longer fear tomorrow.
16. I am blessed.
17. This too shall pass.
18. I control how I feel.
19. I am willing to do what it takes to make positive changes.
20. The future is mine, if I choose to take it.
21. I am indestructible.
22. This moment is awesome.
23. Positive thinking is part of who I am now.
24. Today is the first day of my new life.
25. Everything happens for a reason that serves me.

Every step that I take to move forward allows me to grow stronger by the day.

30 Ways to Think More Positively

After years of having a fixed, negative mindset, it's tough to change one's ways. But with practice, you can create a more positive outlook on life. Here's 30 ways to practice thinking more positively.

1. When talking, replace negative words with positive words. Instead of saying "This is too hard", say "I can do this" or "I accept this challenge".

2. When thinking, use empowering words; those that make you feel strong, happy, motivated and in control.

3. Journal your thoughts. Celebrate your successes. Document and analyze the losses. Find where you went wrong and plan to do better next time. Learn from your mistakes.

4. Counter each negative thought with multiple positive thoughts. When you catch yourself having negative thoughts, take a moment to think two or three positive thoughts.

5. Go somewhere that brings you peace and happiness. This might be a nature walk, a quiet place like a museum that is visually appealing, an area where you listen to music, a park where you can watch kids and pets play happily. As often as possible, visit this place where you feel peace and happiness.

6. Practice positive affirmations. The more you practice, the easier it will become.

7. Forgive yourself for missteps. It happens. The important this is not to dwell on them and keep moving forward.

8. Surround yourself with positive people.

9. Add inspiring visuals and colors to your home and work space.

10. Look at things from a different point of view. When you can see both sides, you can eliminate a lot of negatively.

11. Laugh aloud and often. There's always something to laugh about. Smiling and laughing releases 'feel good' endorphins in the body.

12. Remember your "why". Why you are trying to be more positive, what your goals are, how things will be better once you meet your goals, etc.

13. Practice gratitude. When you're feeling thankful, you'll feel more positive.

14. Live in the moment. Stop worrying about yesterday or what's coming. Do what you can do today to get one step closer to reaching your goals.

15. Indulge yourself occasionally. You are working hard to be a more positive person. You deserve a small reward.

16. Carry a funny photo with you. Save a funny video on your phone to give you a boost when you're feeling down.

17. Look at each challenge as an opportunity to grow. Strive for excellence.

18. Relax. Sometimes you just need to step back, breathe deep and relax to get the good vibes flowing again.

19. Get physically active to release more 'feel good' endorphins.

20. Believe in yourself. The only thing keeping you from succeeding is your own negative thoughts. Stop getting in your own way.

21. Stop making excuses and laying blame. Take responsibility for your actions and make the choice to do better next time.

22. Observe your thought patterns. Are there certain times of the day when you're feeling more negative? What can you do to make those times more positive?

23. Ask yourself, does this really matter? Will it matter next week or next month? If not, let it go. This called not sweating the small stuff.

24. Practice proper posture. Standing or sitting up with the back straight, shoulders back and chin up will help the mind and body feel better.

25. Be kind to others. Compliment a stranger. Do something nice for coworker or friend. Call a family member you haven't talked to in a while.

26. Read something inspiring every day. Follow those who inspire you most and see what they do each day to make like the best it can be. Follow their lead.

27. Dance and sing. It doesn't matter if you have two left feet or can't carry a tune. Crank up the music and give it all you've got.

28. Look for the positive. Even in the worst of situations, there's always something positive if you just look for it.

29. Have a personal mantra. No matter what it is, these will be the words you live by each day that reminds you to be positive.

30. Meditate, do yoga, concentrate on your breathing and relaxing your mind.

Challenges I Will Overcome

Life is full of challenges. This worksheet is designed to help you work through how you'll overcome the challenges you face.

The Challenge I'm Currently Facing

_____
_____
_____
_____
_____

The Obstacle(s) Standing in My Way

Obstacle #1:
_____
_____

How I Will Overcome It
_____
_____
_____
_____

People & Tools I'll Need to Help Me with This
_____
_____
_____

Obstacle #2:
_____

How I Will Overcome It

_____
_____
_____
_____

People & Tools I'll Need to Help Me with This

_____
_____
_____
_____

Obstacle #3:

_____
_____

How I Will Overcome It

_____
_____
_____
_____

People & Tools I'll Need to Help Me with This

_____
_____
_____
_____

Previous Challenges That May Resurface & How I Will Handle Them

_____
_____
_____

Previous Challenges That May Resurface & How I Will Handle Them

More Thoughts on This Challenge:

Top Characteristics of Happy People

Ever wonder why some people always seem happy when others do not? It's all about how you view things. Below are the top characteristics of happy people.

Happy people:

- Practice gratitude and show their appreciation.
- Are genuinely nice to others
- Are open and honest
- Are cooperative
- Smile when they mean it
- Are well-adjusted and appreciate simple pleasures
- Surround themselves with other happy people
- Are spontaneous and adventurous
- Are good listeners
- Have fewer expectations, and fewer disappointments
- Don't judge others and don't let judgmental people affect them.
- Actively try to be happy each day
- Are resilient. They bounce back from obstacles and failures.
- Help others when they can
- Spend time doing nothing
- Choose meaningful conversations over small talk
- Stay connected with those they love
- Look for the positive in everything
- Regularly unplug from technology, if only for a few hours a week.
- Try to maintain a healthy mind and body through proper eating, exercise, and rest.

- Laugh loud and laugh often, fully enjoying the moment
- Like themselves
- Have self-control
- Are optimistic
- Are spiritual
- Lead a balanced life
- Embrace their creativity

S.M.A.R.T. Goals Worksheet

Goals give us something to visualize, to work towards. They keep us from becoming stagnant in life. This worksheet is designed to help you set smart goals.

Today's Date: _____   Date to Achieve Goal By: _____

Date Goal Achieved: _____

Specific: What exactly do you want to accomplish? What is the desired result. Why do you want to achieve it? How do you plan to achieve it? Be specific.

_____
_____
_____
_____
_____
_____
_____
_____
_____
_____
_____
_____
_____
_____
_____
_____
_____
_____
_____

Measurable: How will you know when you've accomplished this goal? How are you going to measure your progress? How often are you going to measure and document your progress?

_____
_____
_____
_____
_____
_____
_____
_____
_____
_____
_____
_____

Achievable: Is this goal achievable? What skills, tools, and resources do you need to make it happen? Do you have these? If not, how will you get them?

_____
_____
_____
_____
_____
_____
_____
_____
_____
_____
_____
_____

Relevant: Is this goal relevant to your life? Will it help you reach your life goals quicker? Will it benefit your life in some way? How is it relevant? Be specific.

_____
_____
_____
_____
_____
_____
_____
_____
_____

Timely: When do you want to achieve this goal? Is this target date reasonable?

_____
_____
_____

Progress / Notes

Month 1	Month 2	Month 3	Month 4	Month 5	Month 6

Every step that I take to move forward allows me to grow stronger by the day.

Today I Am Grateful For...

This worksheet is designed to help you practice gratitude. Make as many copies as you'd like. The more you practice gratitude, the happier your life will be.

Something that happened to me recently that I am grateful for:
_____
_____
_____
_____
_____
_____
_____

Someone who is always there for me and I really appreciate:
_____
_____
_____

Someone I look up to and why:
_____
_____
_____
_____
_____
_____

The best thing that happened today:
_____
_____
_____
_____

Something that has made my life easier:
_____
_____
_____
_____
_____
_____

Someone I love spending time with and why:
_____
_____
_____
_____
_____
_____

I smiled or belly laughed today because:
_____
_____
_____
_____
_____
_____

A song that makes me happy
_____
_____

Something I was able to do for someone else that made me happy:
_____
_____
_____

Something that has changed my life for the better in the past year and how it has impacted my life.
___
___
___
___
___
___
___
___

I'm looking forward to:
___
___
___
___
___
___

Simple pleasures I enjoy:
___
___
___
___

Something or someone that has inspired me and how:
___
___
___
___
___
___
___
___

Positive Thinking To Help Situational Depression

Negativity is often an overwhelming element of situational depression. For millions of people with this type of depression, the key to begin breaking free is to change the situation, when possible, and/or the way the situation is viewed.

What situation is contributing to or causing my depression?
_____
_____
_____
_____

Is the situation a result of my actions or choices? Explain.
_____
_____
_____
_____

What are the positive things I've learned due the experience?
_____
_____
_____
_____

If I could do it over again, this is what I would do differently:
_____
_____
_____

Is negative self-talk making my depression worse? Give examples:

_____
_____
_____
_____

I can change the negative thoughts and self-talk into positives like these:

_____
_____
_____
_____

I can alleviate my stress and depression by focusing on the positives such as:

_____
_____
_____
_____

When situations are not a result of my actions or choices and I have limited control over things, I need to take these steps to maintain a positive mindset:

_____
_____
_____
_____

If I need additional help staying positive or fighting back the depression, I can count on and contact these friends and professionals:

_____
_____

25 Positive Thinking Affirmations

Affirmations are simple reminders to our subconscious that tells it to stay positive and focused on reaching our goals. They are meant to be used for ourselves, not for others. Affirmations can create more appreciation for the things we have and are surrounded with. They can bring more joy and happiness to our lives.

When creating your affirmations, there are a few things to keep in mind.

- Including the words "I am" in your affirmations bring power to your statement.
- Positively state what you want, not what you don't want.
- Keep your statements short and specific.
- Include words that show action or emotion
- Before stating your affirmation, take a deep breath and focus on what you're saying.
- Be grateful for what you have, the people in your life and your surroundings.
- Let go of the past. You can't change it so don't waste time thinking on it.
- Celebrate your 'wins'.

Below are 25 positive thinking affirmations to get you started.

1. I can do better, just by deciding to do so.
2. Life is what I make of it.
3. I can.
4. I am above negative thoughts and actions.
5. Happiness is a choice. I choose it.
6. Today, I let go of old habits and take up new ones.
7. I am conquering obstacles every day.
8. I am seeing a positive in every situation.
9. My thoughts are becoming more positive each day.
10. Life is getting better all the time.
11. I am turning into the person I always wanted to be.
12. Thinking positive is starting to feel more natural to me.
13. My optimism is altering my reality.
14. I am at peace with my past and looking forward to the future.
15. I no longer fear tomorrow.
16. I am blessed.
17. This too shall pass.
18. I control how I feel.
19. I am willing to do what it takes to make positive changes.
20. The future is mine, if I choose to take it.
21. I am indestructible.
22. This moment is awesome.
23. Positive thinking is part of who I am now.
24. Today is the first day of my new life.
25. Everything happens for a reason that serves me.

Every step that I take to move forward allows me to grow stronger by the day.

30 Ways to Think More Positively

After years of having a fixed, negative mindset, it's tough to change one's ways. But with practice, you can create a more positive outlook on life. Here's 30 ways to practice thinking more positively.

1. When talking, replace negative words with positive words. Instead of saying "This is too hard", say "I can do this" or "I accept this challenge".

2. When thinking, use empowering words; those that make you feel strong, happy, motivated and in control.

3. Journal your thoughts. Celebrate your successes. Document and analyze the losses. Find where you went wrong and plan to do better next time. Learn from your mistakes.

4. Counter each negative thought with multiple positive thoughts. When you catch yourself having negative thoughts, take a moment to think two or three positive thoughts.

5. Go somewhere that brings you peace and happiness. This might be a nature walk, a quiet place like a museum that is visually appealing, an area where you listen to music, a park where you can watch kids and pets play happily. As often as possible, visit this place where you feel peace and happiness.

6. Practice positive affirmations. The more you practice, the easier it will become.

7. Forgive yourself for missteps. It happens. The important this is not to dwell on them and keep moving forward.

8. Surround yourself with positive people.

9. Add inspiring visuals and colors to your home and work space.

10. Look at things from a different point of view. When you can see both sides, you can eliminate a lot of negatively.

11. Laugh aloud and often. There's always something to laugh about. Smiling and laughing releases 'feel good' endorphins in the body.

12. Remember your "why". Why you are trying to be more positive, what your goals are, how things will be better once you meet your goals, etc.

13. Practice gratitude. When you're feeling thankful, you'll feel more positive.

14. Live in the moment. Stop worrying about yesterday or what's coming. Do what you can do today to get one step closer to reaching your goals.

15. Indulge yourself occasionally. You are working hard to be a more positive person. You deserve a small reward.

16. Carry a funny photo with you. Save a funny video on your phone to give you a boost when you're feeling down.

17. Look at each challenge as an opportunity to grow. Strive for excellence.

18. Relax. Sometimes you just need to step back, breathe deep and relax to get the good vibes flowing again.

19. Get physically active to release more 'feel good' endorphins.

20. Believe in yourself. The only thing keeping you from succeeding is your own negative thoughts. Stop getting in your own way.

21. Stop making excuses and laying blame. Take responsibility for your actions and make the choice to do better next time.

22. Observe your thought patterns. Are there certain times of the day when you're feeling more negative? What can you do to make those times more positive?

23. Ask yourself, does this really matter? Will it matter next week or next month? If not, let it go. This called not sweating the small stuff.

24. Practice proper posture. Standing or sitting up with the back straight, shoulders back and chin up will help the mind and body feel better.

25. Be kind to others. Compliment a stranger. Do something nice for coworker or friend. Call a family member you haven't talked to in a while.

26. Read something inspiring every day. Follow those who inspire you most and see what they do each day to make like the best it can be. Follow their lead.

27. Dance and sing. It doesn't matter if you have two left feet or can't carry a tune. Crank up the music and give it all you've got.

28. Look for the positive. Even in the worst of situations, there's always something positive if you just look for it.

29. Have a personal mantra. No matter what it is, these will be the words you live by each day that reminds you to be positive.

30. Meditate, do yoga, concentrate on your breathing and relaxing your mind.

Challenges I Will Overcome

Life is full of challenges. This worksheet is designed to help you work through how you'll overcome the challenges you face.

The Challenge I'm Currently Facing

_____
_____
_____
_____
_____

The Obstacle(s) Standing in My Way

Obstacle #1:
_____
_____

How I Will Overcome It
_____
_____
_____
_____

People & Tools I'll Need to Help Me with This
_____
_____
_____
_____

Obstacle #2:
_____

How I Will Overcome It

_____
_____
_____
_____

People & Tools I'll Need to Help Me with This

_____
_____
_____
_____

Obstacle #3:

_____
_____

How I Will Overcome It

_____
_____
_____
_____

People & Tools I'll Need to Help Me with This

_____
_____
_____
_____

Previous Challenges That May Resurface & How I Will Handle Them

_____
_____
_____

Previous Challenges That May Resurface & How I Will Handle Them

More Thoughts on This Challenge:

Top Characteristics of Happy People

Ever wonder why some people always seem happy when others do not? It's all about how you view things. Below are the top characteristics of happy people.

Happy people:
- Practice gratitude and show their appreciation.
- Are genuinely nice to others
- Are open and honest
- Are cooperative
- Smile when they mean it
- Are well-adjusted and appreciate simple pleasures
- Surround themselves with other happy people
- Are spontaneous and adventurous
- Are good listeners
- Have fewer expectations, and fewer disappointments
- Don't judge others and don't let judgmental people affect them.
- Actively try to be happy each day
- Are resilient. They bounce back from obstacles and failures.
- Help others when they can
- Spend time doing nothing
- Choose meaningful conversations over small talk
- Stay connected with those they love
- Look for the positive in everything
- Regularly unplug from technology, if only for a few hours a week.
- Try to maintain a healthy mind and body through proper eating, exercise, and rest.
- Laugh loud and laugh often, fully enjoying the moment
- Like themselves
- Have self-control

- Are optimistic
- Are spiritual
- Lead a balanced life
- Embrace their creativity

S.M.A.R.T. Goals Worksheet

Goals give us something to visualize, to work towards. They keep us from becoming stagnant in life. This worksheet is designed to help you set smart goals.

Today's Date: _____   Date to Achieve Goal By: _____

Date Goal Achieved: _____

Specific: What exactly do you want to accomplish? What is the desired result. Why do you want to achieve it? How do you plan to achieve it? Be specific.

_____
_____
_____
_____
_____
_____
_____
_____
_____
_____
_____
_____
_____
_____
_____
_____
_____
_____
_____
_____

Measurable: How will you know when you've accomplished this goal? How are you going to measure your progress? How often are you going to measure and document your progress?

_____
_____
_____
_____
_____
_____
_____
_____
_____
_____

Achievable: Is this goal achievable? What skills, tools, and resources do you need to make it happen? Do you have these? If not, how will you get them?

_____
_____
_____
_____
_____
_____
_____
_____
_____
_____

Relevant: Is this goal relevant to your life? Will it help you reach your life goals quicker? Will it benefit your life in some way? How is it relevant? Be specific.
_____
_____
_____
_____
_____
_____
_____
_____
_____

Timely: When do you want to achieve this goal? Is this target date reasonable?
_____
_____
_____

Progress / Notes

Month 1	Month 2	Month 3	Month 4	Month 5	Month 6

Every step that I take to move forward allows me to grow stronger by the day.

Today I Am Grateful For...

This worksheet is designed to help you practice gratitude. Make as many copies as you'd like. The more you practice gratitude, the happier your life will be.

Something that happened to me recently that I am grateful for:
_____
_____
_____
_____
_____
_____
_____

Someone who is always there for me and I really appreciate:
_____
_____
_____

Someone I look up to and why:
_____
_____
_____
_____
_____
_____

The best thing that happened today:
_____
_____
_____
_____

Something that has made my life easier:
_____
_____
_____
_____
_____
_____

Someone I love spending time with and why:
_____
_____
_____
_____
_____
_____

I smiled or belly laughed today because:
_____
_____
_____
_____
_____
_____

A song that makes me happy
_____
_____

Something I was able to do for someone else that made me happy:
_____
_____
_____

Something that has changed my life for the better in the past year and how it has impacted my life.
_____
_____
_____
_____
_____
_____
_____
_____
_____

I'm looking forward to:
_____
_____
_____
_____
_____
_____

Simple pleasures I enjoy:
_____
_____
_____
_____

Something or someone that has inspired me and how:
_____
_____
_____
_____
_____
_____
_____
_____

Positive Thinking To Help Situational Depression

Negativity is often an overwhelming element of situational depression. For millions of people with this type of depression, the key to begin breaking free is to change the situation, when possible, and/or the way the situation is viewed.

What situation is contributing to or causing my depression?
_____
_____
_____
_____

Is the situation a result of my actions or choices? Explain.
_____
_____
_____
_____

What are the positive things I've learned due the experience?
_____
_____
_____
_____

If I could do it over again, this is what I would do differently:
_____
_____
_____

Is negative self-talk making my depression worse? Give examples:

_____
_____
_____
_____

I can change the negative thoughts and self-talk into positives like these:

_____
_____
_____
_____

I can alleviate my stress and depression by focusing on the positives such as:

_____
_____
_____
_____

When situations are not a result of my actions or choices and I have limited control over things, I need to take these steps to maintain a positive mindset:

_____
_____
_____
_____

If I need additional help staying positive or fighting back the depression, I can count on and contact these friends and professionals:

_____
_____
_____

25 Positive Thinking Affirmations

Affirmations are simple reminders to our subconscious that tells it to stay positive and focused on reaching our goals. They are meant to be used for ourselves, not for others. Affirmations can create more appreciation for the things we have and are surrounded with. They can bring more joy and happiness to our lives.

When creating your affirmations, there are a few things to keep in mind.

- Including the words "I am" in your affirmations bring power to your statement.
- Positively state what you want, not what you don't want.
- Keep your statements short and specific.
- Include words that show action or emotion
- Before stating your affirmation, take a deep breath and focus on what you're saying.
- Be grateful for what you have, the people in your life and your surroundings.
- Let go of the past. You can't change it so don't waste time thinking on it.
- Celebrate your 'wins'.

Below are 25 positive thinking affirmations to get you started.

1. I can do better, just by deciding to do so.
2. Life is what I make of it.
3. I can.
4. I am above negative thoughts and actions.
5. Happiness is a choice. I choose it.
6. Today, I let go of old habits and take up new ones.
7. I am conquering obstacles every day.
8. I am seeing a positive in every situation.
9. My thoughts are becoming more positive each day.
10. Life is getting better all the time.
11. I am turning into the person I always wanted to be.
12. Thinking positive is starting to feel more natural to me.
13. My optimism is altering my reality.
14. I am at peace with my past and looking forward to the future.
15. I no longer fear tomorrow.
16. I am blessed.
17. This too shall pass.
18. I control how I feel.
19. I am willing to do what it takes to make positive changes.
20. The future is mine, if I choose to take it.
21. I am indestructible.
22. This moment is awesome.
23. Positive thinking is part of who I am now.
24. Today is the first day of my new life.
25. Everything happens for a reason that serves me.

Every step that I take to move forward allows me to grow stronger by the day.

30 Ways to Think More Positively

After years of having a fixed, negative mindset, it's tough to change one's ways. But with practice, you can create a more positive outlook on life. Here's 30 ways to practice thinking more positively.

1. When talking, replace negative words with positive words. Instead of saying "This is too hard", say "I can do this" or "I accept this challenge".

2. When thinking, use empowering words; those that make you feel strong, happy, motivated and in control.

3. Journal your thoughts. Celebrate your successes. Document and analyze the losses. Find where you went wrong and plan to do better next time. Learn from your mistakes.

4. Counter each negative thought with multiple positive thoughts. When you catch yourself having negative thoughts, take a moment to think two or three positive thoughts.

5. Go somewhere that brings you peace and happiness. This might be a nature walk, a quiet place like a museum that is visually appealing, an area where you listen to music, a park where you can watch kids and pets play happily. As often as possible, visit this place where you feel peace and happiness.

6. Practice positive affirmations. The more you practice, the easier it will become.

7. Forgive yourself for missteps. It happens. The important this is not to dwell on them and keep moving forward.

8. Surround yourself with positive people.

9. Add inspiring visuals and colors to your home and work space.

10. Look at things from a different point of view. When you can see both sides, you can eliminate a lot of negatively.

11. Laugh aloud and often. There's always something to laugh about. Smiling and laughing releases 'feel good' endorphins in the body.

12. Remember your "why". Why you are trying to be more positive, what your goals are, how things will be better once you meet your goals, etc.

13. Practice gratitude. When you're feeling thankful, you'll feel more positive.

14. Live in the moment. Stop worrying about yesterday or what's coming. Do what you can do today to get one step closer to reaching your goals.

15. Indulge yourself occasionally. You are working hard to be a more positive person. You deserve a small reward.

16. Carry a funny photo with you. Save a funny video on your phone to give you a boost when you're feeling down.

17. Look at each challenge as an opportunity to grow. Strive for excellence.

18. Relax. Sometimes you just need to step back, breathe deep and relax to get the good vibes flowing again.

19. Get physically active to release more 'feel good' endorphins.

20. Believe in yourself. The only thing keeping you from succeeding is your own negative thoughts. Stop getting in your own way.

21. Stop making excuses and laying blame. Take responsibility for your actions and make the choice to do better next time.

22. Observe your thought patterns. Are there certain times of the day when you're feeling more negative? What can you do to make those times more positive?

23. Ask yourself, does this really matter? Will it matter next week or next month? If not, let it go. This called not sweating the small stuff.

24. Practice proper posture. Standing or sitting up with the back straight, shoulders back and chin up will help the mind and body feel better.

25. Be kind to others. Compliment a stranger. Do something nice for coworker or friend. Call a family member you haven't talked to in a while.

26. Read something inspiring every day. Follow those who inspire you most and see what they do each day to make like the best it can be. Follow their lead.

27. Dance and sing. It doesn't matter if you have two left feet or can't carry a tune. Crank up the music and give it all you've got.

28. Look for the positive. Even in the worst of situations, there's always something positive if you just look for it.

29. Have a personal mantra. No matter what it is, these will be the words you live by each day that reminds you to be positive.

30. Meditate, do yoga, concentrate on your breathing and relaxing your mind.

Challenges I Will Overcome

Life is full of challenges. This worksheet is designed to help you work through how you'll overcome the challenges you face.

The Challenge I'm Currently Facing

_____
_____
_____
_____
_____

The Obstacle(s) Standing in My Way

Obstacle #1:
_____
_____

How I Will Overcome It
_____
_____
_____
_____

People & Tools I'll Need to Help Me with This
_____
_____
_____
_____

Obstacle #2:
_____

How I Will Overcome It

_____
_____
_____
_____

People & Tools I'll Need to Help Me with This

_____
_____
_____
_____

Obstacle #3:

_____
_____

How I Will Overcome It

_____
_____
_____
_____

People & Tools I'll Need to Help Me with This

_____
_____
_____
_____

Previous Challenges That May Resurface & How I Will Handle Them

_____
_____
_____

_____
_____

Previous Challenges That May Resurface & How I Will Handle Them
_____
_____
_____
_____
_____
_____
_____

More Thoughts on This Challenge:
_____
_____
_____
_____
_____
_____
_____
_____
_____
_____
_____
_____

Top Characteristics of Happy People

Ever wonder why some people always seem happy when others do not? It's all about how you view things. Below are the top characteristics of happy people.

Happy people:
- Practice gratitude and show their appreciation.
- Are genuinely nice to others
- Are open and honest
- Are cooperative
- Smile when they mean it
- Are well-adjusted and appreciate simple pleasures
- Surround themselves with other happy people
- Are spontaneous and adventurous
- Are good listeners
- Have fewer expectations, and fewer disappointments
- Don't judge others and don't let judgmental people affect them.
- Actively try to be happy each day
- Are resilient. They bounce back from obstacles and failures.
- Help others when they can
- Spend time doing nothing
- Choose meaningful conversations over small talk
- Stay connected with those they love
- Look for the positive in everything
- Regularly unplug from technology, if only for a few hours a week.
- Try to maintain a healthy mind and body through proper eating, exercise, and rest.
- Laugh loud and laugh often, fully enjoying the moment
- Like themselves
- Have self-control

- Are optimistic
- Are spiritual
- Lead a balanced life
- Embrace their creativity

S.M.A.R.T. Goals Worksheet

Goals give us something to visualize, to work towards. They keep us from becoming stagnant in life. This worksheet is designed to help you set smart goals.

Today's Date: _____ Date to Achieve Goal By: _____

Date Goal Achieved: _____

Specific: What exactly do you want to accomplish? What is the desired result. Why do you want to achieve it? How do you plan to achieve it? Be specific.

_____
_____
_____
_____
_____
_____
_____
_____
_____
_____
_____
_____
_____
_____
_____
_____
_____
_____
_____

Measurable: How will you know when you've accomplished this goal? How are you going to measure your progress? How often are you going to measure and document your progress?

_____
_____
_____
_____
_____
_____
_____
_____
_____
_____
_____

Achievable: Is this goal achievable? What skills, tools, and resources do you need to make it happen? Do you have these? If not, how will you get them?

_____
_____
_____
_____
_____
_____
_____
_____
_____
_____
_____

Relevant: Is this goal relevant to your life? Will it help you reach your life goals quicker? Will it benefit your life in some way? How is it relevant? Be specific.

_____
_____
_____
_____
_____
_____
_____
_____
_____
_____

Timely: When do you want to achieve this goal? Is this target date reasonable?

_____
_____
_____

Progress / Notes

Month 1	Month 2	Month 3	Month 4	Month 5	Month 6

www.ingramcontent.com/pod-product-compliance
Lightning Source LLC
LaVergne TN
LVHW071321191224
799503LV00012B/710